This book belongs to:

Hipster Santa
Travels the World at Christmas
Coloring Book

Sandy Mahony
Mary Lou Brown

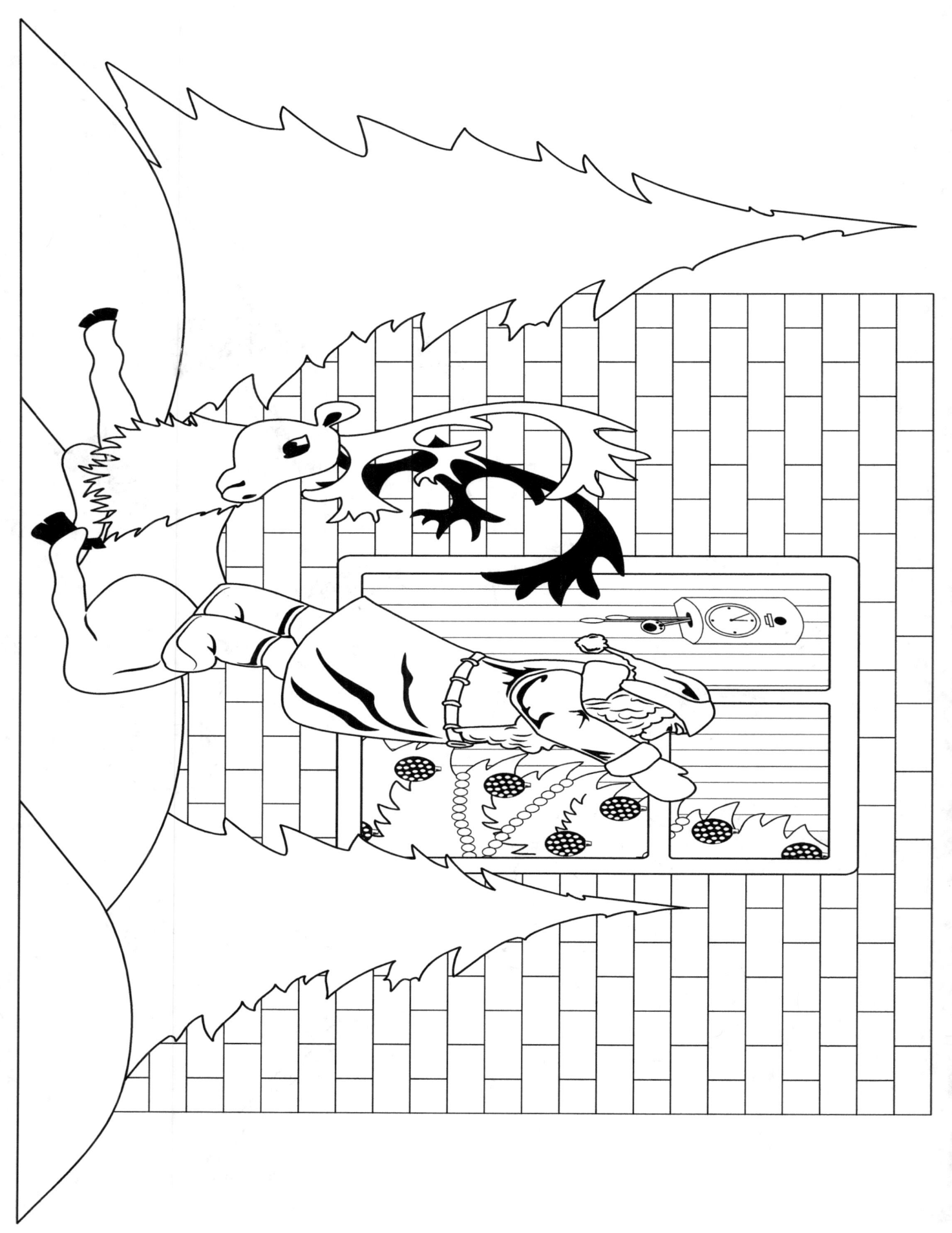

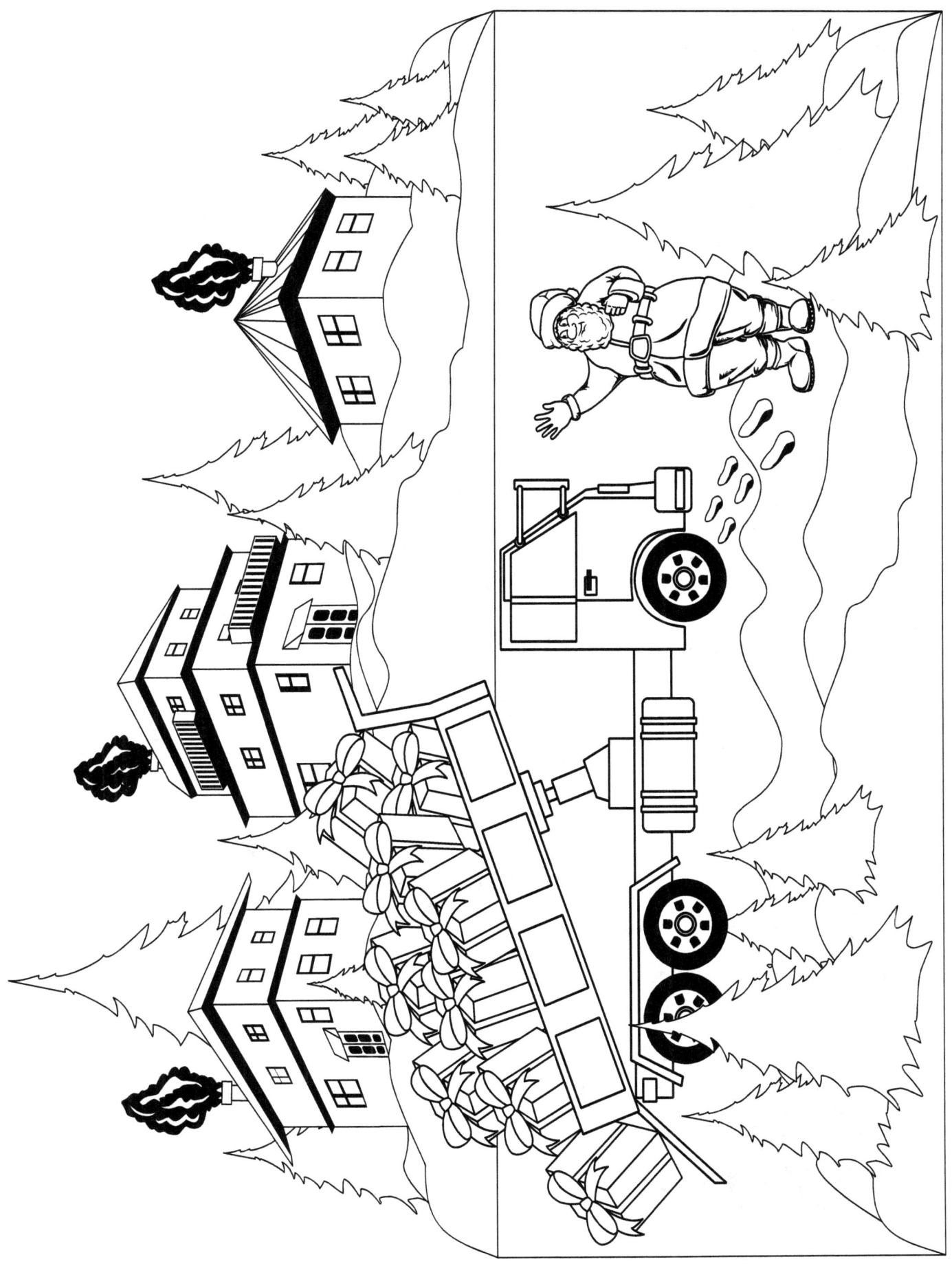

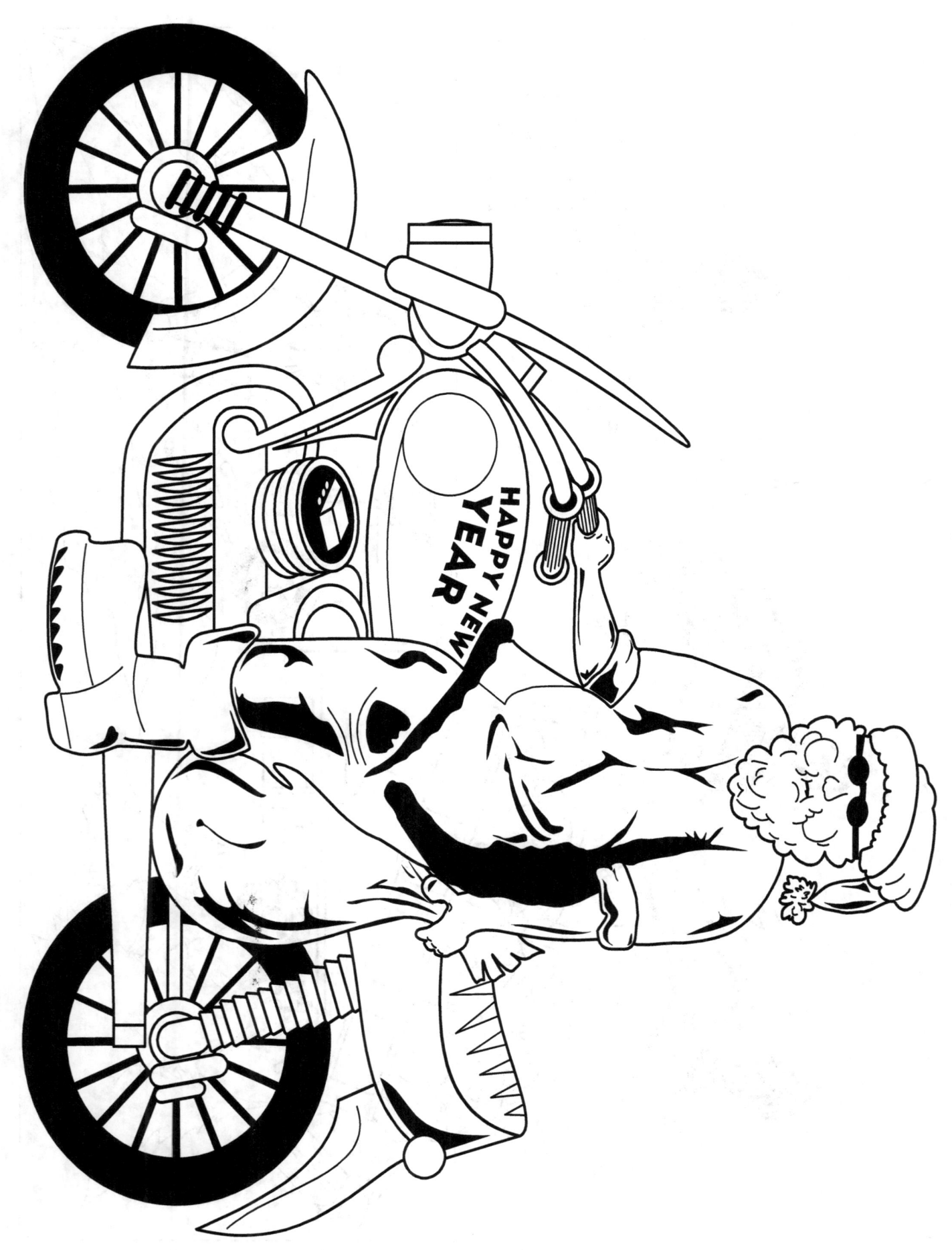

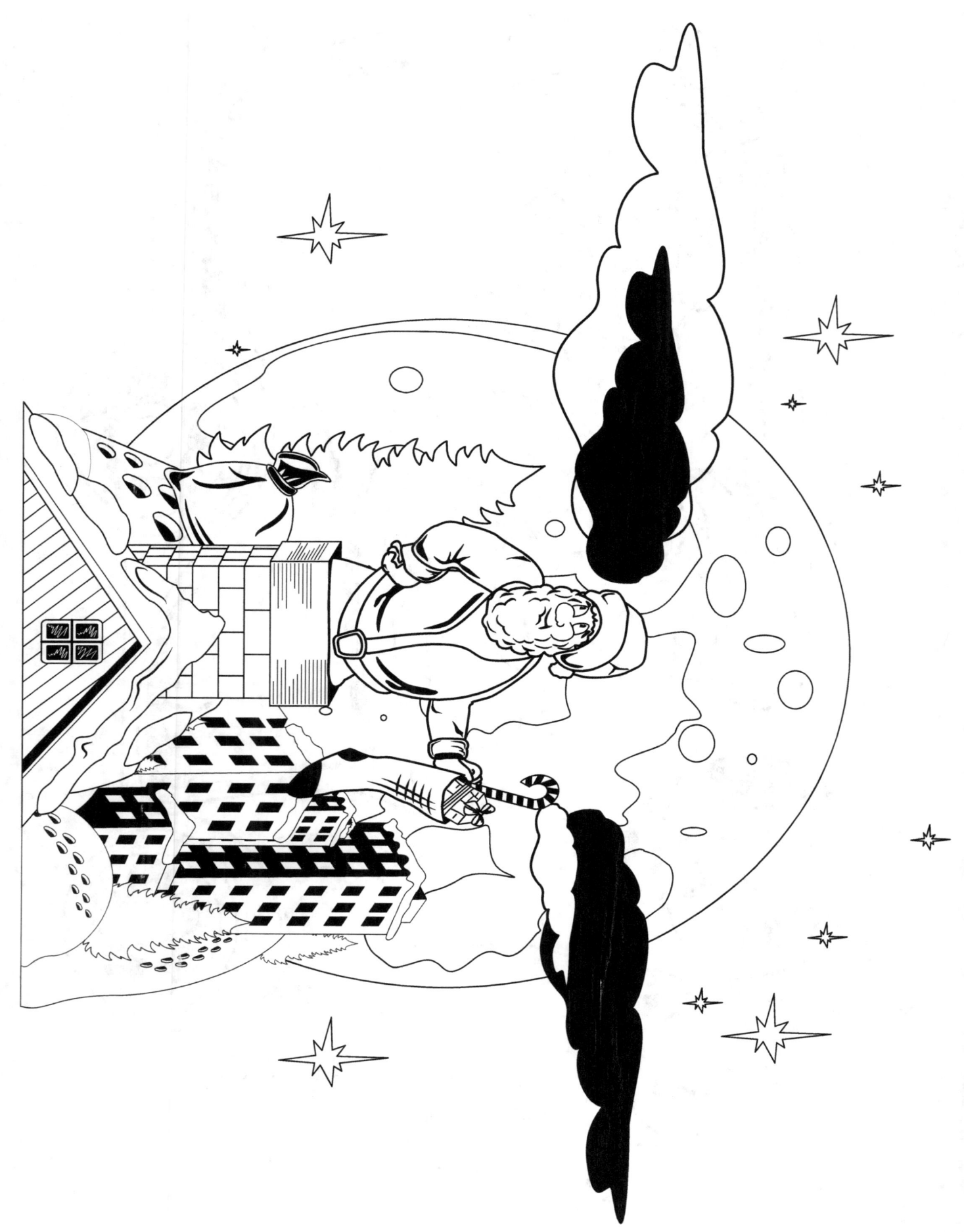

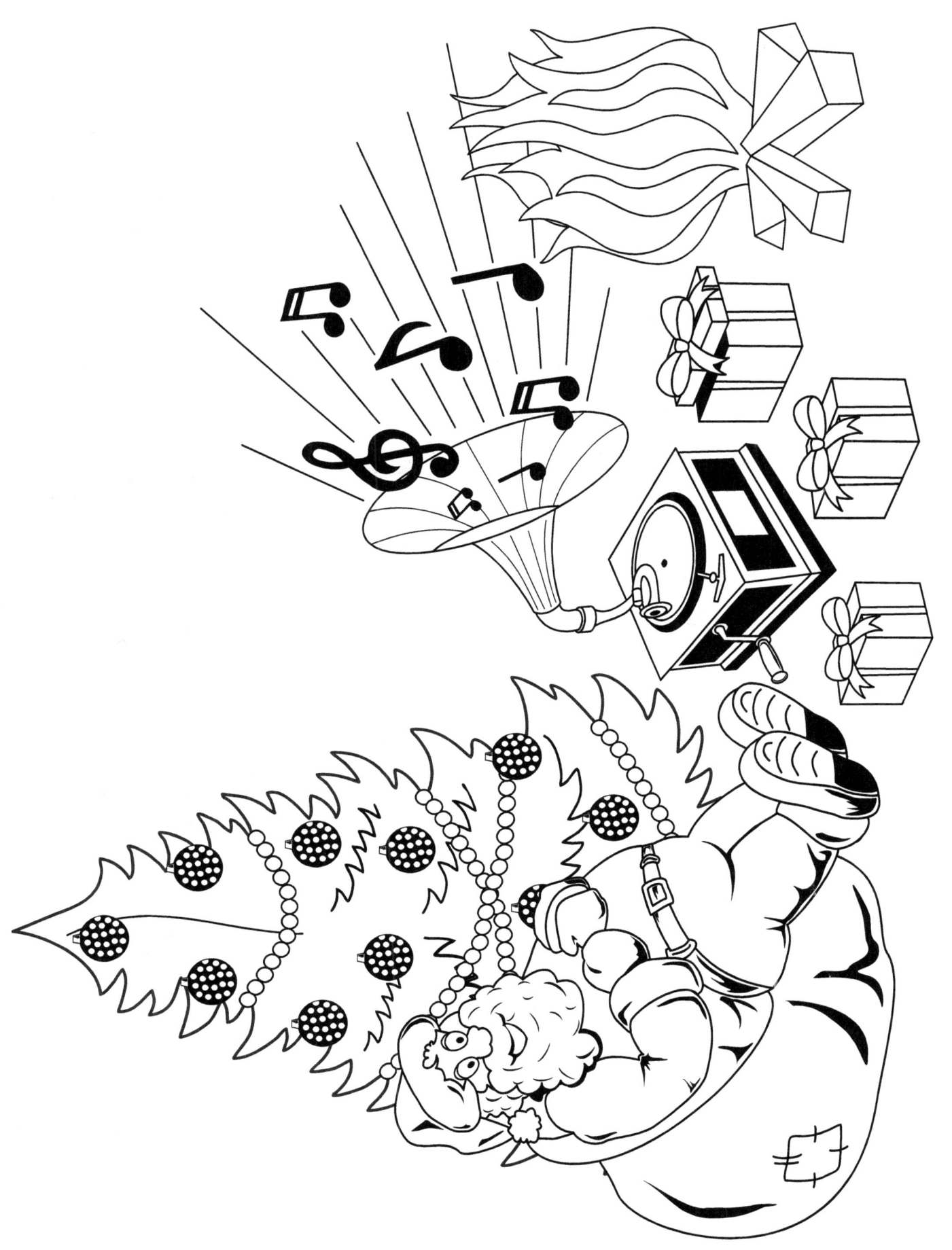

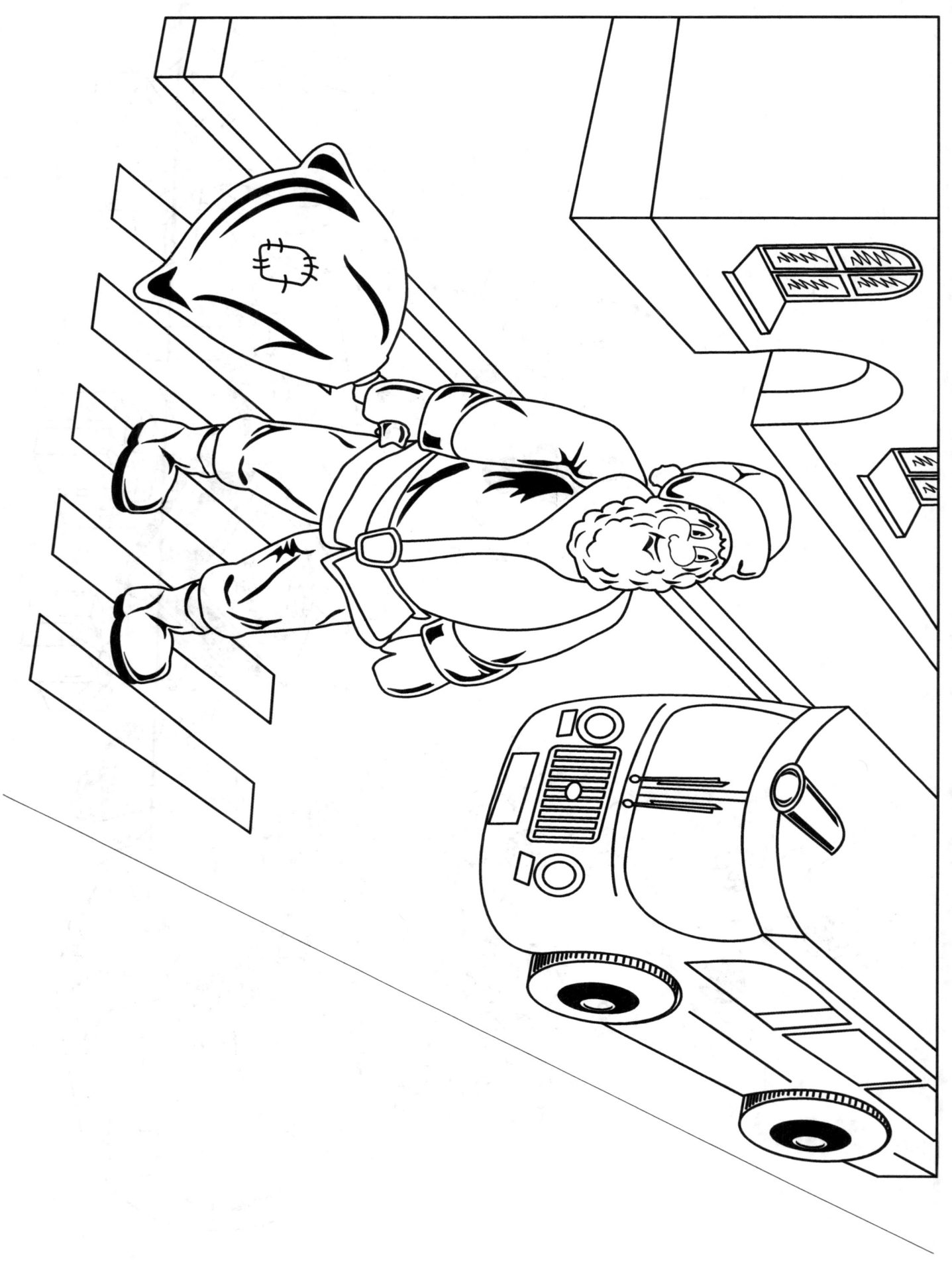

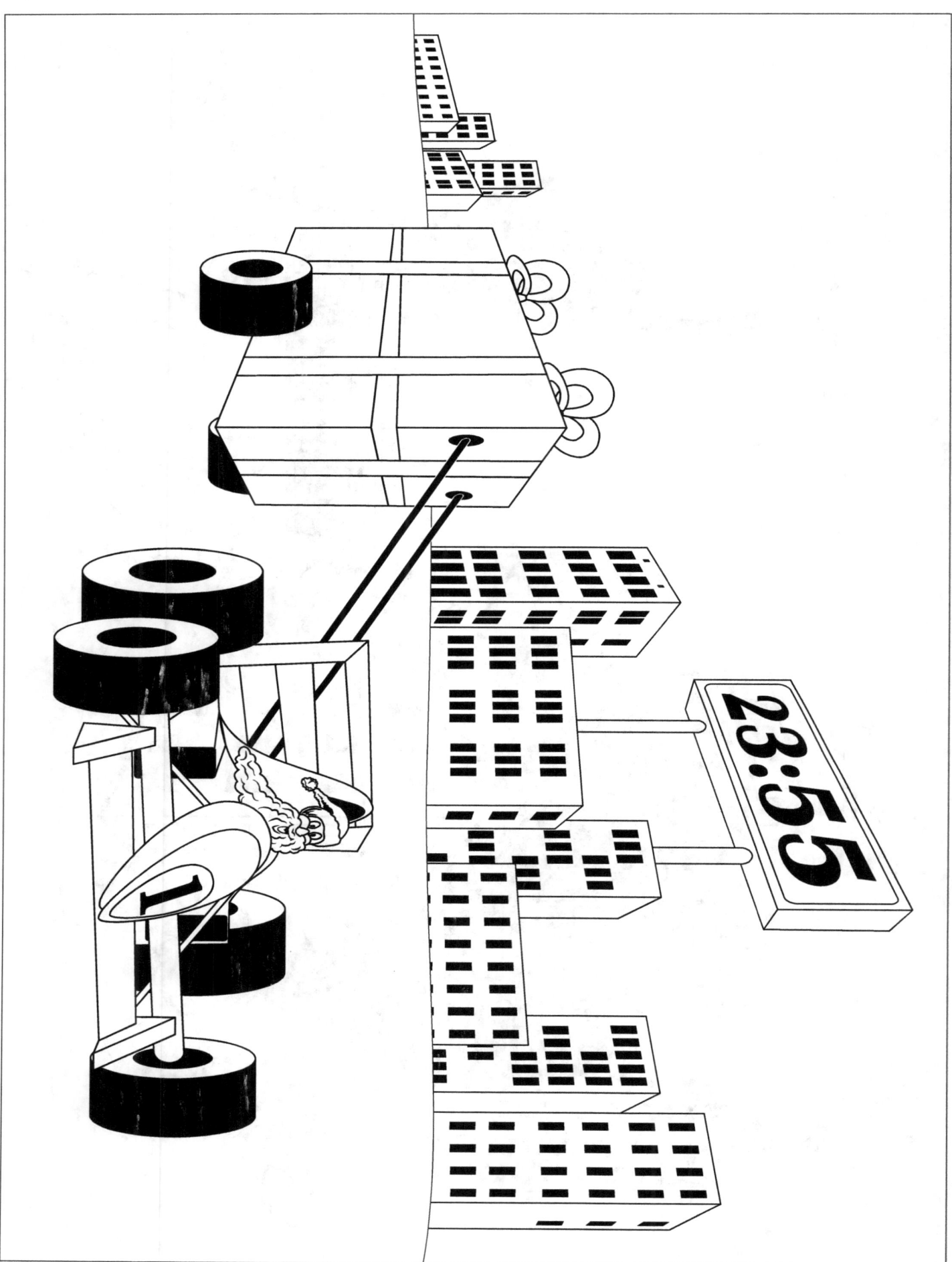

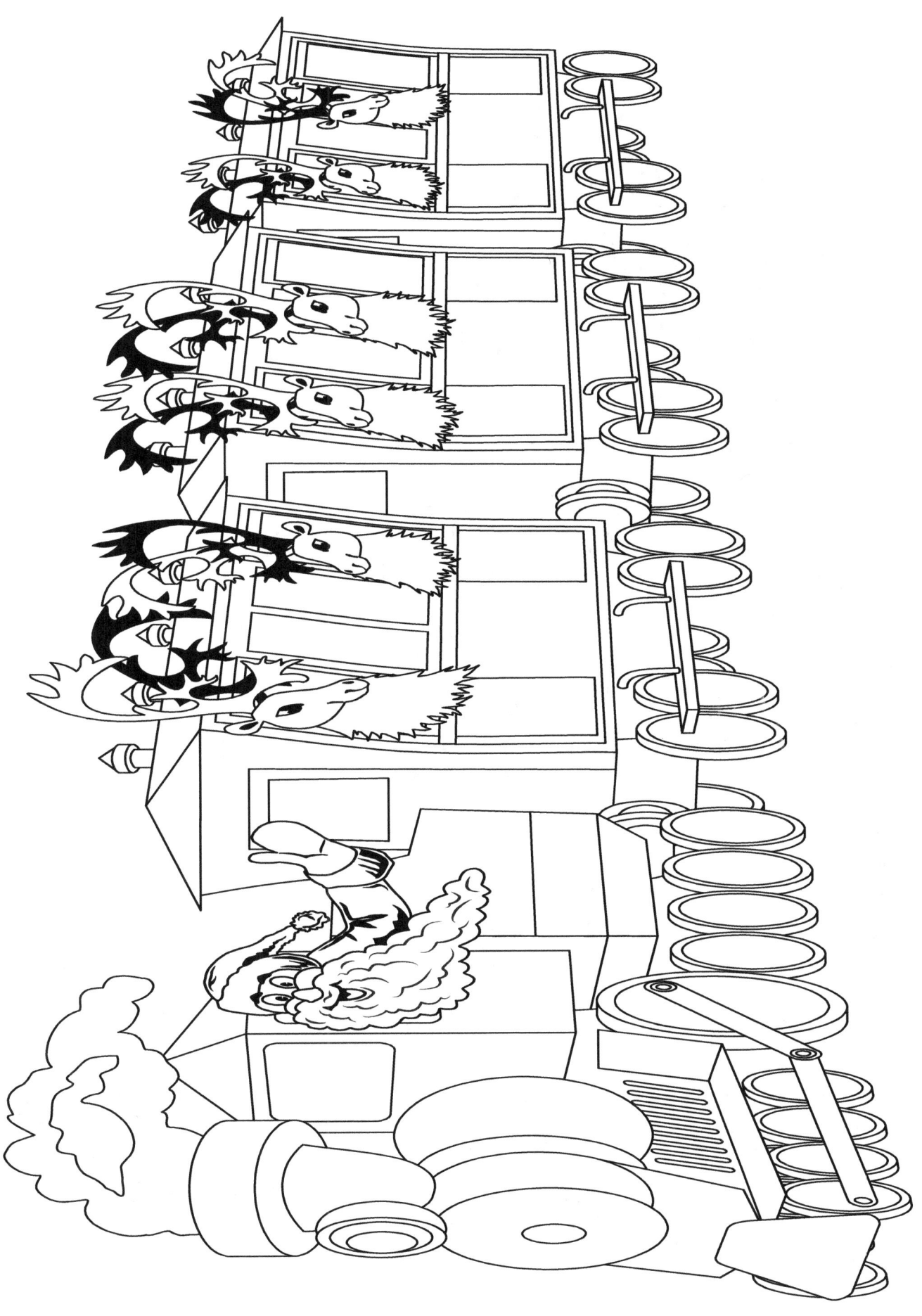

www.ingramcontent.com/pod-product-compliance
Lightning Source LLC
Chambersburg PA
CBHW081800280526
45789CB00008B/2939

9 781540 454720